FISHING IN
LAKES AND PONDS

JUDY MONROE PETERSON

rosen publishing's
rosen central®

New York

To Belle, Jasmine, and their dad—all love to eat fish!

Published in 2012 by The Rosen Publishing Group, Inc.
29 East 21st Street, New York, NY 10010

Library of Congress Cataloging-in-Publication Data

Peterson, Judy Monroe.
Fishing in lakes and ponds / Judy Monroe Peterson.—1st ed.
        p. cm.—(Fishing: tips & techniques)
Includes bibliographical references and index.
ISBN 978-1-4488-4597-2 (library binding)
ISBN 978-1-4488-4603-0 (pbk.)
ISBN 978-1-4488-4734-1 (6-pack)
1. Fishing—Juvenile literature. I. Title.
SH445.P48 2012
799.1'1—dc22

                                                                        2010044137

Manufactured in Malaysia

CPSIA Compliance Information: Batch #S11YA: For further information, contact Rosen Publishing, New York, New York, at 1-800-237-9932.

CONTENTS

*f*ishing is a popular and relaxing outdoor sport in North America and around the world. Millions of people enjoy fishing in a wide variety of lakes and ponds. A lake is a body of water entirely surrounded by land. Many natural lakes are expanded sections of rivers or creeks. Some river curves become separated and are called oxbow lakes. Some are made from water in the form of melting snow or rain that runs off from the surrounding area. A pond is a body of still freshwater and is smaller than a lake. Natural underwater springs create many ponds, and sometimes people construct others.

Anglers catch freshwater fish in lakes and ponds. Unlike the salty oceans and seas, inland lakes and ponds contain little or no salt. Many people like small fish called panfish, which are sunfish (sunnies), crappies, bluegills, and perch. Favorite larger fish are walleye, northern pike, and muskellunge (muskies).

Freshwater fish are readily accessible to people of all ages across North America. Some anglers make frequent, short trips to nearby lakes and ponds, or they might take longer trips to large lakes for catching a particular fish. People can angle in lakes and

ponds using simple equipment such as a cane pole. Many people use rods, reels, and other equipment, which allow for a variety of angling methods. The method of fishing determines the type of equipment used to catch fish.

Casting baited hooks from shore on lakes and ponds is an inexpensive way to catch fresh fish. Fishing lakes exist in many cities or within short distances across North America.

Fishing takes patience, knowledge, and skill. Anglers need different strategies and bait to outwit freshwater fish. They use baits based on the habits of a particular type of fish. Zones are layers of different temperatures of water in a lake or pond that separate different fish habitats. Small fish are usually found in the shallow, warmer water zone, while larger fish inhabit the open water zone. Some fish live only in the deeper, colder water zone.

State and provincial fishing laws regulate the seasons of the year for fishing. The laws vary from state to state. Sometimes states set aside lakes only for releasing caught fish. All anglers need to know and follow regulations. Most states and provinces require anglers to buy a fishing license. State and federal laws control fishing to avoid overharvesting and extinction of freshwater fish. To manage their fish populations, states have seasons for each type of fish. People can legally keep a particular fish during its season.

By buying licenses and paying taxes on fishing equipment, anglers provide money to the states to enforce fishing laws, manage fishing and boating access of lakes and ponds, and improve the habitat of fish. State agencies also work to destroy invasive fish. The federal government offers many freshwater fishing opportunities through its National Wildlife Refuge fishing programs. The National Fish Hatchery System allows fishing at or near many hatcheries.

Fishing can be enjoyed alone or shared with family and friends. People might combine fishing with boating, camping, picnicking, hiking, or viewing wildlife. Some anglers like the challenge of finding and landing big fish and then releasing them back into the lake or pond after taking a photograph. Other people catch fish to preserve and save as trophies. People enjoy eating fish because the meat is tasty and nutritious.

CHAPTER 1

ANGLER SAFETY AND RESPONSIBILITIES

*A*nglers should prepare to be safe and comfortable in the outdoors and near and on water. Bad weather can suddenly develop without warning. People can get painful sunburns or get caught on a fishhook. Safe anglers help prevent accidents. An important step to take before fishing is for anglers to let someone know where they will be fishing and when they will return. In addition, they should keep a telephone number handy for the resource management in the area so that if an accident happens, they can get help.

Weather and Water Safety

Anglers need to stay informed about the weather forecast and be prepared for severe weather. They should also pay attention to any unexpected wind,

These young anglers are wearing flotation life vests. If they should fall into the water, these vests will keep them afloat, with their mouth and nose above the surface.

rain, and lightning. It is a good idea for them to take a waterproof radio to listen to weather forecasts when they are on long trips. Thick, gray clouds rolling in or sudden gusts of cold air signal an approaching storm. If a storm approaches, people in boats should head for shore. They need to put their rod down, get out of the water, and take cover. They should stay away from tall trees and move to low ground in case there are nearby lightning strikes. Wearing rainwear and other gear can help keep people from getting wet and chilled.

When they are on boats, anglers need to keep a safe speed and watch wave conditions. They need to look out for sandbars, rocks, and submerged trees that could snag their boats. It is important for fishers to stay away from litter that could cut or entangle their fishing equipment or the boat motor.

Most states require that all anglers wear flotation gear while on the water. These life vests are lightweight and do not restrict people's movements. Flotation devices should be worn at all times, whether anglers are on a boat or a dock.

Fishers should also be sure that docks are sturdy before they begin fishing from them. Before wading into water, anglers need to check for sharp drop-offs and areas of powerful undercurrents. They also need to be careful to take one step at a time because it can be slippery along banks. Wading with rubber boots or tennis shoes protects the feet from sharp pieces of debris such as broken glass.

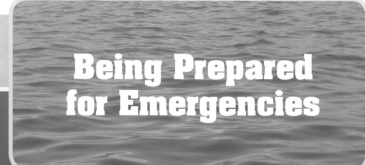

Being Prepared for Emergencies

In an emergency, people might need to know how to treat simple injuries or get help. Having a basic first-aid kit allows them to get immediate treatment for minor injuries. Treating injuries right away lessens the chance of wounds becoming infected and helps keep fishers from ending their trip too soon. People can buy a basic first-aid kit for fishing trips or make their own by using a small, waterproof container. A first-aid kit should contain bandages of different sizes, antibiotic ointment, safety scissors, gauze, medical tape, and cleansing towelettes (wet wipes) or sanitizing gel. An over-the-counter pain reliever such as acetaminophen can help lessen the pain from an injury or headache. Other items that can come in handy are tweezers, a small bottle of water to rinse wounds, and a cold pack to help reduce swelling caused by an injury. Extra insect repellent and sunblock lotion are also good to include in the kit.

Safety Tips

An important rule is always walk, not run, around water shorelines. Fishers should wear flotation devices when they are on docks or on the banks of lakes or ponds. A boat must have a U.S. Coast Guard–approved flotation or inflatable life jacket for each person aboard. Inflatable life jackets keep people face up with their head above the water and afloat. These devices are available in many shapes, colors, and sizes.

When fishing, people should wear a billed hat or cap and polarized sunglasses. The hat protects an angler from the sun's hot rays and from getting hooked if another angler makes a bad cast. Wearing polarized sunglasses protects anglers' eyes and helps them see into the water to spot fish. Fishers should protect their lips with sunscreen. They need to cover their face, neck, ears, back of hands, legs, and other skin exposed to the sun with a waterproof sunscreen that has a sun protection factor (SPF) of fifteen or higher. Sunburns are more likely to happen during the middle of the day when the sun is the hottest and reflects off the water. Using insect repellents before going on the water helps ward off mosquitoes, flies, and bees.

Fishers should pack some cold water and other healthy drinks. While fishing, it is important to take breaks to stay hydrated and prevent heatstroke (effects of too much heat). Many sodas (soft drinks) contain caffeine and increase the likelihood of becoming dehydrated. Energy bars, fruit, nuts, and other healthy snacks are also good to bring.

Before going fishing, savvy fishers check the weather forecast and wear the right clothing. When fishing in warm or hot weather, it is a good idea to bring raingear as the weather can become rainy. Anglers should bring warmer clothing in case the weather turns cold. When fishing in cold weather, anglers will want to dress in layers and wear a warm hat. To keep dry, the outer layer needs to be waterproof. Underneath, people can wear layers of comfortable, warm clothing.

Using Equipment Safely

Safe use of fishing equipment can help anglers avoid accidents. People should point their rod toward the sky when they are walking. When casting, fishers need to watch for people behind, on the sides, and in front. An overhead cast is safer than side casts. Overhead casts can help anglers avoid crossing or tangling their fishing line with that of someone else.

Hooks are sharp and require careful attention when baiting and removing them. Fishers should not grab a fish where it is hooked. Fish wiggle when hooked, and the hook can get caught in the hand. It is important to always handle fish carefully and avoid the mouth and spine of fish. Some fish have sharp fins on their backs. Perch and other fish have sharp gill covers. Gills are openings on the side that allow the fish to breathe.

Having equipment ready to go is a smart course of action. People should keep their fishing knives sharp and cover the blade when the knife is not in use. They can clean their rods, reels, hooks, lures, and other fishing equipment regularly. Fishers should watch for rough spots on rods because they will cause extra wear on the line. The line may then break as an angler is reeling in a fish!

Regulations and Sportsmanship

Fishers need to check out where they plan to fish. They should not fish in areas where it is not permitted. Areas might be off limits to fishing to protect wildlife, vegetation, or the safety of people. Shorelines of some lakes and ponds are owned privately or by an angling club.

Every state and province requires anglers ages twelve and older to buy a fishing license. This license can be purchased from the local

A fishing license must be purchased in most states for people who are ages twelve and older. Some people save their first fishing license as a keepsake.

department of natural resources, sporting good stores, bait shops, or the state's department of natural resources or on the department's Web site. Anglers must know and follow the fishing laws for the state. The laws include limits, legal hours, license requirements, seasons, any special regulations, and allowable gear. Fishing regulations differ for each state. People can obtain the regulations wherever they purchase fishing licenses.

Many states have restrictions such as use of lures, hooks, and bait for certain waters. States control the number of fish that can be taken in one day and the seasons for fishing in lakes and ponds. The limits may be different for each type of fish and the time of year. Other laws require that people take only fish of a specific size. Anglers are encouraged to release fish they catch if the fish will not be eaten. Mature fish will reproduce so that there is a next generation.

Anglers need to exhibit good sportsmanship whether or not people are watching them. For example, it is important to follow the license requirements for the exact number and size of fish that have been caught. When anglers fish from boats, they should not crowd other anglers who are also fishing. Fishers should keep some distance between them and someone else's spot.

Fishers show good sportsmanship when they are respectful of other people and their property. They must not fish from private land without the permission of the landowner. It is illegal (against the law) to trespass. Anglers need to respect the rights of others. They might see or meet other people enjoying the land and wildlife, such as hikers, bird watchers, and campers. Fishers need to respect swimmers, boaters, and other anglers so that these people can also enjoy their activities on the water.

Before leaving the lake or pond, people should pack their bait containers and any trash off the water or shoreline and dispose of them properly. Throwing garbage or fishing tackle into the water is a bad idea. Fish, birds, and small animals can swallow discarded plastic lures, fishing line, and hooks and then die. Anglers need to treat public and private property as if it were their own. Public lands belong to everyone and should be protected for everyone's use or access.

Some lakes have dangerous chemical pollution that can affect fish and make them unsafe to eat. Every state has publications that report which fishing waters are polluted.

Catching and Eating Safe Fish

Edible freshwater fish can contain a variety of contaminants (poisons) that may make those who eat them sick. The state departments of natural resources publish on their Web sites lists of lakes that have pollution, such as lead and mercury, which may contaminate fish caught from that lake. Other chemicals such as polychlorinated biphenyls (PCBs), chlordane, and DDT have been banned in the United States. However, they last a long time in the mud beneath the water. Small fish eat the dangerous chemicals that have settled in the mud. Bigger fish, such as walleyes, northern pikes, and muskies, eat smaller fish and the contaminants that are in them. Anglers should follow the public postings that recommend which fish and how much of that fish can be safely eaten.

CHAPTER 2

TACKLE AND OTHER EQUIPMENT

Anglers need three basic tools to catch fish in lakes and ponds: a rod, a reel, and fishing line. They also need hooks on the end of the fishing line to attach their live bait and lures, as well as bobbers, weights, and sinkers or floats. Fishing equipment is called tackle. Most of these items fit inside a tackle box that has a handle for carrying. People organize and store their equipment in a tackle box and take it when they go fishing. The type of equipment needed by the anglers depends on the type of fish they plan to catch.

Rods and Reels

Most people start by selecting a rod and reel. Rods are tapered poles of various thicknesses and lengths. Materials such as fiberglass, graphite, and carbon fiber are popular choices

It is easy to fish from shore with the basic tools of a rod, a casting reel, and a line tipped with a hook or lure.

for rods because they are strong, lightweight, and flexible. Many anglers use rods that are 5 to 7 feet (1.5 to 2.1 meters) long. A shorter rod is best for shorter, more accurate casts. A longer rod allows for casting farther out into the water.

The action of fishing rods varies. People who are after panfish require fast-action rods that are short and bend at the tip. Slow-action rods bend closer to the reel and handle. These stronger, longer, and more flexible rods are often used to catch large walleye, northern pike, and muskies. Many people choose medium-action rods when fishing for various types of fish in lakes and ponds. These rods bend in the middle.

Reels store unused line and allow anglers to control the line and the attached bait or lure when they are fishing. People release line when casting and retrieve line when turning the reel's handle. Most reels have a device that controls the tension (tightness) of the line on the spool while fishing. Spinning and spin-casting are the most popular types of reels for fishing in lakes and ponds.

Spinning reels have an open-faced spool mounted on the reel. The spool does not turn when the line is cast or retrieved. The line comes off the open end of the spool while the fisher is casting. Spinning reels have a handle and a bail to retrieve line or allow line to come off the spool. The bail winds the line around the spool. The spool turns only when the fish pulls on the line hard enough to overcome the drag.

Cane Pole Fishing

A popular way to fish is with a cane pole, which is often made from dried bamboo or a sapling tree. Anglers attach strong duck decoy line to the pole. Cane poles do not have reels. They are inexpensive and a good choice for beginning anglers for fishing in lakes and ponds. At about 8 feet (2.4 m) in length, cane poles are often longer than standard rods for lakes and ponds. A cane pole allows people to feel the slightest nibble of a fish. A disadvantage of this type of fishing is that anglers cannot fish a distance away. All the casts must be close. Because people cannot cast a long distance with a cane pole, they place the bait in precise spots. This practice allows them to target close areas with pinpoint accuracy (right next to a lily pad, for example). Pole fishing is efficient with the use of bobbers for panfish.

Spin-casting reels have a hood or cap covering a spool. Line comes off the spool and passes through a hole in the hood or cap. Fishers use a push-button to release line from the spool during casting and turn a handle to retrieve line. A device winds the line evenly onto the spool and prevents it from tangling.

Line, Hooks, Bait, and Lures

Once anglers have a rod and reel, they need line and a hook. Monofilament lines are popular for people who fish in lakes and ponds. These single, strong strands of plastic fibers are used on spinning and spin-casting reels and come in many thicknesses and lengths. Fish do not

Catching walleyes with an artificial wood or plastic lure tipped with a live minnow is very effective. Anglers often have favorite baits that work best for them.

see them because they are clear or tinted to match the color of water. Lightweight line of 6-pound test works well for panfish. Six pounds (2.72 kilograms) of pressure can be put on the line before it breaks. Anglers use heavier, stronger lines to catch large walleye, muskies, and northern pike.

People can choose from hundreds of sizes and shapes of steel hooks. Hooks are strong and very sharp, and range in size from 1 (large) to 22 (small). People fishing in lakes and ponds typically find that hook sizes 14 to 16 work well for most fish. However, a size 6 to 10 hook is best for panfish. Hooks can be used individually or attached to artificial plastic, rubber, metal, or wood lures. Many fisheries specify that fishers should use barbless hooks, especially if a catch-and-release policy is in effect. A barb holds the hook in place when a fish is caught, but is difficult to remove without damaging the fish.

People use natural or artificial bait to catch fish. Panfish, walleyes, muskies, and northern pike feed on smaller fish and other small animals, such as crayfish, waterfowl, and rodents. When fishing, people place small fish such as minnows on their hook. Other natural bait includes worms, leeches, insects, frogs, corn, cheese, and popcorn. To attract and catch panfish, minnows and worms should be threaded on a hook. If threaded correctly, the minnow will swim and only the end of the worm will dangle in the water.

Unlike live bait, lures can be reused. Most lures are designed to look and act like natural bait. Lures come in thousands of shapes and sizes. Most are made of plastic, metal, or wood. Metal spinners and spoons are favorite lures. Spinners spin in the water and reflect light as the lure is retrieved. The noise, light, and motion attract fish. Spoons jerk and wobble when they are pulled through the water. Anglers use spoons weighing 1/16 ounce (1.8 grams) for small panfish. Larger spoons work for walleyes, northern pike, and muskies. Crank baits and poppers are also popular lures when fishing on lakes and ponds. By tying feathers and string to a steel hook, artificial flies, grubs, and insects are made that resemble the original animal. These lures are usually called flies.

Other Equipment

Anglers often attach a lead sinker (weight) near the hook so that their bait sinks to the correct depth in a lake or pond. When fish are found at a certain depth, fishers can put a bobber on the line. Bobbers float on

Over time, many anglers experiment with different types of equipment for freshwater fishing. They often have a tackle box to store small gear such as sinkers and hooks.

water, but wiggle or bob down when a fish nibbles or strikes at the bait or lure. Using a bobber allows the angler to place the line at a greater distance from the shoreline or boat.

Some types of fish such as northern pike and muskie have sharp teeth that easily cut the line. To overcome this, people use steel leaders. Leaders are thin wire lines that attach between a swivel on the end of the line and the hook. Swivels allow the bait attached to the leader to turn freely, which keeps the line from twisting.

Other equipment that people often carry is a small pocket knife and nail clippers. These tools come in handy to cut fishing line and other gear. In addition, anglers can remove hooks from the mouth or stomach of a caught fish with forceps or pliers. A bait box is useful for storing bait.

Some people fish on the water from small boats, canoes, and rubber rafts. A watercraft provides access to deep areas of a lake or to a submerged (beneath the surface of the water) island. To locate the hot spots for fishing, anglers often use a lake map. The topography of the bottom of a lake or pond is important to know because it can identify where fish are resting or likely to feed. Additional electronic devices such as depth finders and global positioning systems (GPS) are also useful. Depth finders use sonar to help locate fish. Then they display the location of fish on a screen. Once fish are found, people use GPS coordinates to mark the exact location for future fishing.

CHAPTER 3

HOW TO FISH

Panfish, walleye, northern pike, and muskies are found in lakes and ponds throughout most of the United States and southern Canada. To be successful, anglers need to learn how to correctly identify their fish. They also must learn the habitat and behavior of the different types of fish. Habits (predictable animal behaviors) include finding comfortable water temperatures, feeding, resting, spawning, and hiding from predators under cover.

Water temperature greatly influences the hunger and activity of fish. They will move to different depths to locate comfortable temperatures. The chances of catching fish increase as people learn more about fish characteristics and feeding habits. Successful fishers are patient and may need to change methods and bait to catch fish while they are on the same trip.

Panfish

Panfish are plentiful across the United States. They weigh as much as 1 pound (450 grams), but usually weigh less. These small fish average 6 to 8 inches (15 to 20 centimeters) in length. Anglers look for panfish in warm shorelines near lily pads, logs, sunken trees, boat

Anglers know to hook panfish when their bobber jiggles, jumps, and then disappears under water. Panfish bite hard on baited hooks and are great fun to catch.

docks, and weeds. The best time to catch panfish is when they feed at early morning and dusk. When spawning in the spring, panfish are hungry and near shore. They also bite well most of the summer and early fall.

Panfish include sunfish, bluegill, crappies, and yellow perch. Pumpkinseed sunfish and bluegill live near warm shorelines. Pumpkinseeds have a small mouth and an orange breast and belly. The ear flap has a bright red or orange spot. Bluegills have a small mouth and a light yellow belly. The upper body is olive green, dark bands circle the back, and they have a dark area near the tail. Sunfish and bluegills eat insects, mollusks, snails, and small fish. Crappies are silvery olive with a high fin on the back and belly. Black crappies have dark-green spots, and dark-green white crappies have bands of dark-green speckles on the body. The diet of crappies and yellow perch includes insects, spiders, snails, worms, fish eggs, and small fish. Yellow perch are long and slender with a large mouth and two top fins. Their golden-yellow body has dark bands down the sides, and their belly is white or yellow. Perch often swim in schools.

Anglers catch panfish using worms or crickets as bait. By weaving the worm on the hook and leaving a little of the tail to dangle, fishers can keep panfish from stealing the bait. Small leeches and artificial insects also work well as bait. Dropping bait into the water while still-fishing is probably the most popular way to catch panfish, but slow trolling and drifting are other common techniques.

To still-fish, fishers use light line weight, small split-shots (weights), small bobbers, and sizes 6- to 10-long shank hooks. When still-fishing, some anglers jiggle the bobber to move the worm around in the water. The movement catches the fish's eye. When a panfish has swallowed the hook, anglers need to set the hook firmly with a hard, quick snap of the wrist.

Walleyes are a popular fish to catch because their white meat is flaky and delicious. If one walleye is caught, more will be in the same area because they swim in schools.

Walleyes

Although walleye inhabit many lakes, Minnesota, Wisconsin, Ohio, Michigan, and much of Canada have the largest populations. Adults typically weigh 1 to 8 pounds (0.4 to 3.6 kg) in the northern states and 15 to 20 pounds (6.8 to 9 kg) in the southern states. The color of walleyes varies, but most are gold-olive with a white belly. They have a dark mark near the tail and a white tip on the lower tail. The large, silvery eyes glow in the dark. Walleyes feed mostly on small fish, insects, crayfish, and worms. They often travel in schools and prefer clear, cool waters with sandy, gravel, or rocky bottoms. To look for food, walleyes swim near rock piles, gravel bars, reefs, and weeds.

When the sun is setting or the water is muddy due to wind, walleyes often school and feed in shallower water. At sunset or during the night, slow trolling with artificial lures or shiners (large minnows) is a successful fishing technique. This method requires a boat with legally placed lights on the bow and stern. Anglers use sonar to find walleyes or trolling lures to catch them in deep water.

Collecting Bait

Worms are excellent bait for panfish. Anglers can collect their own night crawlers by looking for them on the soil with flashlights right after dark. This method works especially well on rainy days. To enhance the collection of night crawlers, some people water their lawns heavily, which drives the worms to the top of the soil. Anglers can find red worms by spading and turning over rich soil. Walleye, northern pike, muskies, and other larger fish eat fry (small fish) and minnows. They will even eat the fry of their own species (type). However, catching and using the fry of game fish as bait is illegal in all states. Using live bait fish, such as minnows, is an effective way to catch fish in lakes and ponds. Although anglers can buy minnows, they can also catch their own. To do this, they need to buy minnow traps. They place bread or corn in the traps, which attracts the minnows.

Walleyes are also caught by still-fishing and drifting. Minnows, jigs with worms, and spinners are the best bait for these methods. Walleyes also go after other bait such as night crawlers and leeches. A 12-pound (5.4-kg) test or less is used for line, along with a sinker so that the hook with bait reaches the bottom of a lake. When a walleye picks up the bait, it slowly swims away. When fishers feel a slight tug on their line, they should release the line until the walleye stops, then quickly reel up the line and set the hook.

Northern Pike

The spear-shaped northern pike is green or black with a white or yellow belly. It is referred to as a northern, a pike, or a northern pike. This fish has white or light yellow bean-shaped spots on its sides with fins that are tipped in orange. Rows of razor-sharp teeth line its mouth. A northern can grow more than 3 feet (1 meter) long and weigh more than 20 pounds (9 kg). Small fish live in warm, shallow lakes and ponds. Larger fish prefer cooler, deep lakes. Anglers can find northerns near thick weeds in clear water. The best time for fishing is during the day, when northern pikes feed. Their diet is mostly fish and sometimes frogs and other water bait. Northern pikes eat both live and dead animals.

Fishing for northerns requires a medium or medium-heavy action rod, 10- to 12-pound (3.6- to 5.4-kg) test line, a 6- or 12-inch (15- or 30-cm) leader, and a slip bobber. Anglers use spinning, spin-casting, or casting to catch northern pikes by trolling fast or casting.

Probably the most effective bait for catching northern pike is a spoon. They are bright, shiny, and made of metal. Spoons can be cast or trolled behind small boats at a fast speed. When a spoon is moved through the water, it wobbles and flutters. A northern sees the moving spoon as live bait and furiously attacks it. Sometimes, the fish will follow the lure for a distance, striking it repeatedly before swallowing it. Fishers should set the hook after the northern has struck at the bait. The spoons can be set with a very stiff or hard jerk because these fish have a hard mouth that can make hook setting difficult.

Using live minnows as bait works well. An interesting way to fish for northern pike in all seasons is by putting a large hook through a dead fish, and then placing a weight on a line that is heavy enough to take the bait to the bottom of a pond or lake. Northern pikes will feed on

Many natural resource departments have fishery biologists who raise game fish such as this muskie. These small fish are called fry. They are released into lakes and ponds to restock a declining fish population.

fish that are on the bottom of a pond or lake. This method works well if the bait is an oily, small fish such as smelt, cisco, or lake herring.

Muskies

Muskies are long and sleek and can be silver, light brown, or light green. They have many dark spots on the body and smaller spots are on the tail. Some muskies have no spots. All have excellent vision. This fish can grow to 60 or 70 pounds (27 or 31 kg) and up to 40 inches (1 m) long in a large lake. Muskies live near weeds in warm, shallow water and deeper, colder water. Their diet is mainly smaller fish, but they eat other live water animals.

Fishing for muskies requires 6 to 8 foot (1.8 to 2.4 m) baitcasting rods with stiff tip action and free-spool casting reels, lines of 20 to 50 pounds (9 to 22.6 kg), leaders, snaps, and swivels. Steel leaders must be used because muskies have very sharp teeth. Most anglers fish for muskies from boats by trolling and casting during the day when the fish are feeding.

When they are caught, muskies put up a strenuous fight. Some anglers fish muskies for the supreme action that it gives when the fish is caught. A large number of muskie anglers fish year after year and release every muskie they catch. They fish for the fun of catching this powerful and challenging fighter with a rod and reel. When casting, a muskie will occasionally follow the lure to the side of the boat. Then it will lie like a large, sunken submarine next to the boat. Suddenly, it will strike the bait if the angler loops the bait next to the boat in a figure-eight motion. Pulling in the vigorously fighting muskie is a thrill that anglers never forget.

CHAPTER 4

APPROACHES TO FISHING AND PREPARING THE CATCH

Some anglers catch and release their fish. Others keep them for eating because they make tasty meals! Fish need to be kept alive as long as possible before filleting or they should be quickly packed on ice. If not kept cold, fish spoils rapidly in warm weather. To keep fish fresh, anglers can let the fish stay in water on hooks called stringers or store them in a basket called a creel. Live wells on some boats can keep caught fish alive until filleted. On land or in boats, fish should be put on ice right away if they cannot be kept alive.

Catch-and-Release Fishing

Once they catch a fish, people can choose to release it. Sometimes they do not

Anglers who fish for sport often practice catch-and-release. Slowly moving the fish back and forth while holding it in water revives the fish. This walleye is being released back into a Minnesota lake.

have a choice. They must follow the regulations of a state and release those fish of stated sizes, which are usually larger, older fish. Laws may require the release of these large fish because they are rare. In addition, they can breed, which increases the fish population of the lake or pond. It is critical to release fish into the lake or pond as soon as possible to give them a good chance to survive.

To release a catch, fishers need to work carefully and quickly to remove the hook. They should try to keep the fish in water at all times, either by holding it or putting it into a net. A good way to remove the hook is to twist and pull it out smoothly, using tools such as long-nosed pliers. When releasing the fish into the water, anglers can cradle its body, grip its tail, and slowly move it back and forth in the water until it starts to swim. The fish is ready to be safely released.

Regulations for Keeping Fish

People need to know the state law for the number of fish that can be stored in their possession at one time. They cannot store more than their legal possession limit. Some state departments of natural resources manage lakes individually. Many lakes have daily fish limits and limits for what size of fish can be kept or released. Other lakes can have minimum size limits on certain types of fish. The department of natural resources often posts these regulations at public accesses and fishing piers.

Every state has regulations on the legal possession limit for the fish of a lake or pond. These laws are designed to prevent overfishing of an area or specific lake. Some regulations are enforced to protect

Fishing licenses pay for state enforcement of fishing regulations. This game warden enforces state fishing laws and checks licenses to make sure people are not fishing out of season.

breeding-age fish so that they can reproduce to help ensure future generations of fish. To learn about the fishing laws of a state, people can go to the state's department of natural resources Web site. The laws are also available every year at fishing license outlets, including county license centers, sporting and hardware stores, and bait shops.

Cleaning and Preserving Fish

People need only a few basic items to scale, gut, and fillet fish. The tools include scissors, a spoon or dull knife for scaling, a fillet knife, containers for the cleaned fish, and newspaper for the discarded offal. A fillet knife is sharp, thin, and flexible. To start, anglers lay the fish on one side. Using scissors, they cut off any sharp fins. Next, they hold the tail or head and remove the scales on each side by scraping the spoon or knife against the skin toward the head. Now they are ready to gut the fish.

To gut, people make a short cut near the anus on the underside of the fish. They move the knife along the belly to the head, spread open the fish, and remove the intestines and other organs. The fins, gills, scales, and intestines can be wrapped in newspaper and discarded.

Next, the head and tail are removed. This leaves two fillets that are joined by the skin. Many people debone the fillets, especially larger ones, by using the tip of the knife to cut and remove the ribs. Then they run their finger along the middle of the fillets to find and remove small bones. Depending on the cooking method to be used, the skin can be left on or removed. The fillets are washed in fresh, cold water and cooked or preserved in the refrigerator or freezer.

The fresher the fish, the better it tastes. Once fish is brought to camp or home and cleaned, people should cook it soon. Or, the fish can be wrapped in plastic and put on ice or refrigerated. It should be eaten

Many resources are available at sporting good stores, libraries, state natural resource departments, and Web sites that can teach people how to fillet and safely prepare fresh fish such as this northern pike.

within forty-eight hours. However, the thin fillets of panfish should be eaten within a day for best flavor.

Cooking Fish

Panfish, walleyes, northern pike, and muskies are tasty and nutritious when they are properly prepared! Fish is lean and lower in fat and calories than meat such as beef. It can be prepared in many healthy ways,

Cooking freshly caught fish over a campfire provides hungry anglers with a delicious meal. People enjoy sharing their experiences while waiting for their fish to cook.

such as grilling, broiling, panfrying, baking, steaming, and microwaving. Panfish are often panfried in a little oil or butter because they cook quickly, within minutes. People also make fish broths, soups, and curries.

Fish cooks fast. It should not be overcooked or it becomes tough and does not taste good. The fillets will break up if they are flipped, turned, or stirred a lot during cooking. Fish is ready to eat when it firms up and gets flaky.

Preserving Fish for Future Eating

Properly frozen fish tastes great. People can use a simple, inexpensive, and efficient way to freeze fish. First, they clean empty milk wax paper containers or plastic jugs. Next, they cut the top of the containers and drop in fresh fish fillets up to two-thirds full. Then they fill the containers with water up to the top of the fillets and freeze them. After approximately six hours, when the water has frozen, people pour in additional water to completely cover any fillets sticking up through the surface of the ice. They also mark the container with the date, type of fish, and number of fillets (or weight). This method of preservation completely surrounds the fillets in ice and keeps the fish fresh for up to a year. To use frozen fish, thaw the package in the refrigerator. Other ways to preserve fish include smoking, dehydrating, and pickling.

CHAPTER 5

FISHING'S EFFECTS ON HABITATS

Responsible anglers protect fish and their habitats. Federal and state governments also work to keep the nation's water and fish healthy and safe. States conduct surveys of fish populations, construct manmade lakes and ponds that provide habitats for fish, and make regulations for fishing. Both state agencies and the U.S. Fish and Wildlife Service share the responsibility of providing fishing recreation. They use hatcheries to help improve fishing by hatching and raising fish for stocking in lakes and ponds. States buy land and build boat and fishing piers for public access to lakes.

Impact of Fishing

Fishing in freshwater lakes and ponds is a popular sport in North America. Hundreds of millions of dollars are generated from buying licenses, sales taxes on purchases of fishing

State fisheries raise fry and then release them into lakes and ponds to ensure future generations of fish. Restocking often occurs when a fish population is greatly decreased due to pollution.

equipment, and from travel and lodging for tourists. States use some of this money to protect and enhance fish populations and manage fish in lakes and ponds. For instance, they might stock fish in lakes and ponds if populations are decreasing.

Although fishing can provide enormous economic benefits to states and local areas, it can negatively impact the environment. For example, overfishing can threaten lakes and ponds. Bigger fish like northern pike and muskies eat smaller fish such as panfish. If anglers take too many large fish, the smaller fish can become overpopulated. Or, anglers might overfish the smaller fish, which reduces the food supply for predator fish.

State governments keep overfishing or overpopulation in check by setting limits on how many specific types of fish can be taken from a lake or pond in one day. Other laws allow fishing only during certain times of the year. For instance, in some areas, people cannot fish during the breeding season because the fish do not reproduce if they are disturbed. In addition, spawning fish are close together and become too easy to catch. Some laws prevent illegal methods of fishing, such as using spears or shocking fish. People cannot use nets that fish get tangled in and then die.

Water Pollution

Water pollution is a problem in North America, threatening the health and safety of people and animals. Clean water is necessary for animals and plants of a lake or pond to live. Power plants that burn coal produce mercury that may be released into nearby water. This practice contributes to the pollution of lakes, ponds, and other water. Mercury is a metal that is naturally found in tiny amounts in soil and rocks. However, large amounts that are poisonous can also be released into the environment from industries that use fossil fuels, such as coal. Mercury is very poisonous, and even small amounts can harm animals. Fish absorb mercury, and over time the level builds up in their bodies. Too much mercury can cause fish and the animals and people who eat the fish to become ill and even die.

Power plants can contribute to water pollution in another way. The heated water that these plants discharge into lakes and other bodies of water reduces the oxygen in the water. Aquatic animals and plants die without enough oxygen to breathe. Heated water can also negatively affect fish that locate their spawning areas by seasonal temperature changes.

Keeping Lead Out of Water

Lead is a naturally occurring metal used in many fishing jigs and sinkers. Over time, exposure in the water to lead can poison fish. Birds that eat fish, such as eagles, loons, and herons, are exposed to lead when they eat fish that have swallowed lead tackle. Anglers can help prevent lead poisoning by using nonlead fishing tackle that is made of steel, tin, tungsten, bismuth, and copper. They should never throw away old fishing gear made of lead into the water, on the shore, or in the trash. Instead, lead items should be brought to the local household hazardous waste collection site. In the past, it was a common practice to paint lures and jigs with lead-based paint. If anglers do not know if their tackle contains lead, they should not put sinkers or jigs in their mouth. Some states restrict or ban the sale and use of lead sinkers and jigs.

Oil and chemical spills poison aquatic animals and plants. Other causes of water pollution include excess fertilizer and animal waste that enters lakes and ponds through rain or runoff. Fertilizers help plants grow. Therefore, they are typically used for crops, lawns, gardens, and golf courses. Large levels of the nutrients in these materials cause rapid growth of small aquatic plants. As more plants grow, more die. Bacteria in the lake or pond use oxygen to break down the dead plants. They also use up the oxygen in the water. Without oxygen in the water, fish will die.

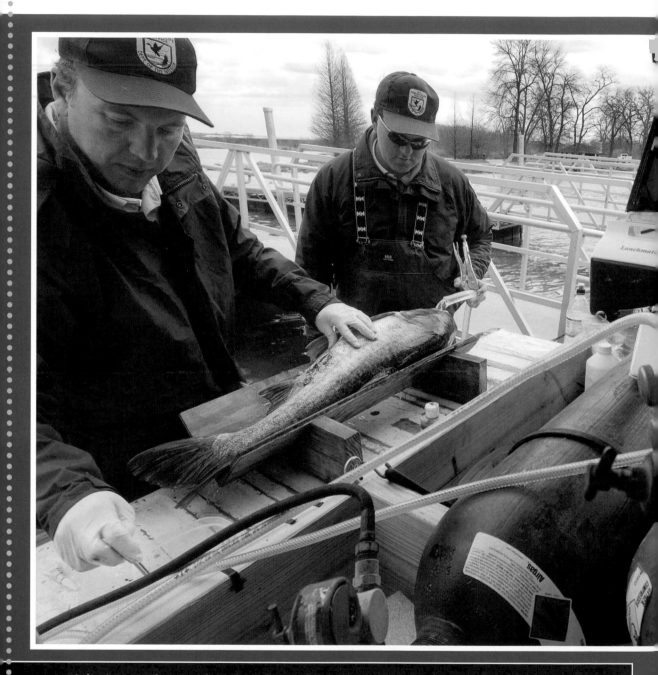

Biologists catch, record, and analyze information about freshwater fish. The biologists seen here have implanted a sonic transmitter into an Asian carp, an invasive species that was found in the Illinois River, to track its movements toward the Great Lakes.

Environmental Responsibilities

Anglers are responsible for protecting fish and keeping their habitats free of pollution. One source of pollution is when people throw trash into the water while they are fishing or on the shore. People on a fishing trip might have old fishing line, weights, rigs, and cans and food wrappers. Used fishing line is especially harmful because fish, birds, and other animals get entangled in it and die. Anglers should put their trash and other people's discarded items into proper containers. Or, they can take the trash home and discard it.

Before fishing, anglers need to make sure they are in approved fishing areas. Some lakes and ponds are off-limits to anglers. Barbless hooks should be used. Fish that are caught with barbless hooks and then released have a better chance of surviving because barbed hooks easily damage a fish's mouth.

Only approved minnows should be bought and used for fishing. Bait shops sell approved bait. People who use goldfish and other fish from their aquarium as bait have caused the spread of invasive fish. These fish have reduced the population of native (existing) fish and damaged their habitat. Goldfish and carp are very harmful because they eat aquatic plants that reduce the level of oxygen in the water. As a result, water temperatures increase and native fish cannot breed. When they eat aquatic plants, goldfish and carp stir up the bottom of lakes and ponds, causing the water to become muddy. Many native fish cannot live in muddy water.

Another invasive species affecting North American lakes is the snake-head fish. This fish comes from Asia and Africa and aggressively preys on local fish and small water animals. It can actually wiggle out of the water and move across land.

People should not release fish from aquariums or water gardens into lakes, ponds, or other water. These fish could carry diseases that are deadly to the native fish. In most states, it is illegal to release nonnative fish into local water. If they are caught, people can be fined. They also may have to pay for the cleanup of the water.

Managing the Nation's Water

To help control water pollution in waterways, the U.S. Congress passed the Clean Water Act in 1972. This law set guidelines that protect the nation's water by controlling the waste that companies put into water. The U.S. Fish and Wildlife Service manages and conserves fish habitats. This agency restores endangered fish and works to stop invasive fish. It also establishes wildlife refuges to protect fish and other animals. The public owns the fish in lakes, ponds, and other water. Federal and state laws control fishing to avoid overfishing and extinction of fish.

The National Fish Hatchery System is part of the U.S. Fish and Wildlife Service. This system protects and conserves fish by restoring fish populations that have decreased or died off in certain lakes. Fish are raised in hatcheries and then released into waters with low populations.

These students are looking at some small freshwater fish inside a national fish hatchery. Millions of young perch, walleyes, and northerns are being raised under the watchful eye of wildlife managers and biologists.

Many anglers support laws to protect fish, improve their habitat, and increase fish populations. They buy fishing licenses, and some pay special taxes on fishing equipment. This money helps pay for enforcement of fishing laws, wildlife management, and conservation programs. Numerous fishers donate their time to help with wildlife management projects, such as improving fish habitats.

Preparing for the Next Fishing Trip

Preparation for the next trip begins as soon as anglers come home. They should clean and safely store their fishing equipment. They also need to check their rods, sharpen hooks, and replace broken items. Many keep a journal or online fishing log and write about what worked well and what did not for each fishing trip. They also note GPS coordinates or draw a map of where they fished.

People have many opportunities to improve their fishing skills and meet other anglers. They can sign up with a fishing club to learn how to fish more skillfully. Most fishing clubs have regular meetings, fishing days, and members who are willing to help beginners. Some clubs organize fishing trips to lakes farther away.

Books, magazines, fishing Web sites, and fishing forums on the Web can help everyone learn more about particular fish, fishing equipment, and methods for future trips. Local tackle and bait shops are great places to learn about fishing in nearby lakes and ponds. Plenty of people who work in these stores enjoy fishing and are often willing to talk about what fishing bait and equipment work best. Spending time outdoors fishing is a great way to have fun, meet interesting people, and catch fish that are delicious to eat!

action The flexibility of or the way a fishing rod bends.

angler A person who fishes with a hook and line.

bait The food used to lure fish to hooks.

carbon fiber A very strong lightweight, artificially made fiber.

chlordane A highly toxic liquid insecticide that was used in the United States.

conservation The protection and preservation of nature.

drag A device that places pressure on the line. Anglers usually adjust the reel's drag after they hook a fish.

drift To fish by trailing a baited hook or lure through the water from a boat that is moving by the wind.

fiberglass A form of glass used for making various products.

freshwater Water without salt.

global positioning system (GPS) A handheld computer that can calculate the exact position using a global positioning satellite.

graphite A form of carbon.

habitat A place where a living thing is naturally found.

hatchery A place where people allow fish eggs to hatch.

invasive A plant or animal outside of its home range.

jig A kind of artificial bait that is jerked up and down through the water.

live well A tank of water on a boat in which caught fish are kept alive.

lure Artificial bait for big freshwater fish.

night crawler A large worm that is active at night on the soil surface.

predator An animal that eats another living animal.

scales The thin, stiff overlapping plates that protect the skin of a fish.

school A group of fish.

season The days of the year when it is legal to fish.

set To jerk the hook firmly into the mouth of a fish.

sonar A device for detecting the presence and location of objects underwater by using sound waves.

spawning When fish breed.

spin-casting Fishing with a light rod and reel that has a device that guides the line around a stationary spool and that can be disengaged to let the line run freely when casting.

taxidermist A professional who mounts trophies.

tension The pressure caused by the action of a pulling force.

trespass To unlawfully enter a person's property.

troll To fish by trailing a baited hook or lure through the water from a boat that is moving by a motor.

trophy A game fish or other animal that is suitable for mounting.

American Sportfishing Association
225 Reinekers Lane, Suite 420
Alexandria, VA 22314
(707) 519-9691
Web site: http://www.asafishing.org
The American Sportfishing Association provides information about
    angling and the sportfishing industry.

Association of Fish and Wildlife Agencies
444 North Capitol Street NW, Suite 725
Washington, DC 20001
(202) 624-7890
Web site: http://www.fishwildlife.org
The Association of Fish and Wildlife Agencies promotes fish manage-
    ment and conservation.

Fresh Water Fishing Hall of Fame and Museum
P.O. Box 690
10360 Hall of Fame Drive
Hayward, WI 54843
(715) 634-4440
Web site: http://www.freshwater-fishing.org
This organization is the international headquarters for education and
    promotion of freshwater fishing.

Future Fisherman Foundation
P.O. Box 6049
McLean, VA 22106
(703) 402-3623
Web site: http://www.futurefisherman.org

The Future Fisherman Foundation works to introduce America's young people to angling and the outdoors.

Ministry of Natural Resources
300 Water Street
Peterborough, ON K9J 8M5
Canada
(800) 667-1940
Web site: http://www.mnr.gov.on.ca/en
The Ministry of Natural Resources manages Ontario's fish and wildlife resources and promotes healthy environments.

National Wildlife Federation
11100 Wildlife Center Drive
Reston, VA 20190-5362
(800) 822-9919
Web site: http://www.nwf.org
The National Wildlife Federation works to protect and restore wildlife habitat in lakes across America.

Ontario Federation of Anglers and Hunters
P.O. Box 2800
Peterborough, ON K9J 8L5
Canada
(705) 748- 6324
Web site: http://www.ofah.org
The Ontario Federation of Anglers and Hunters is a fish and wildlife conservation organization. It focuses on fish hatcheries and improving habitats.

Recreational Boating & Fishing Foundation
500 Montgomery Street, Suite 300
Alexandria, VA 22314
(703) 519-0013
Web site: http://www.rbff.org
The Recreational Boating & Fishing Foundation works to increase
    participation in angling and boating and protect, conserve, and
    restore the nation's aquatic natural resources.

U.S. Fish and Wildlife Service
1849 C Street NW
Washington, DC 20240
(800) 344-9453
Web site: http://www.fws.gov
This government agency manages, conserves, protects, and enhances
    wildlife and their habitats.

Web Sites

Due to the changing nature of Internet links, Rosen Publishing has
developed an online list of Web sites related to the subject of this book.
This site is updated regularly. Please use this link to access the list:

http://www.rosenlinks.com/fish/lake

Arnosky, Jim. *Hook, Line, and Seeker: A Beginner's Guide to Fishing, Boating, and Watching Water Wildlife*. New York, NY: Scholastic Nonfiction, 2005.

Bagur, Daniel. *Where the Fish Are: An Angler's Guide to Fish Behavior*. Camden, ME: McGraw-Hill, 2009.

Burns, Jack, and Rob Kimm. *Pro Tactics: Muskie: Use the Secrets of the Pros to Catch More and Bigger Muskies*. Guilford, CT: Lyons Press, 2008.

Creative Publishing international. *Freshwater Fishing Tips: 300 Tips for Catching More and Bigger Fish*. Chanhassen, MN: Creative Publishing international, 2006.

Dance, Bill. *IGFA's 101 Freshwater Fishing Tips & Tricks*. New York, NY: Skyhorse Publishing, 2007.

Durham, Jason. *Pro Tactics: Panfish: Use the Secrets of the Pros to Catch Bluegill, Crappie, and Perch*. Guilford, CT: Lyons Press, 2008.

Evanoff, Vlad. *How to Make Your Own Fishing Lures: The Complete Illustrated Guide*. Seattle, WA: CreateSpace, 2010.

Ford, Flick. *Fish: 77 Great Fish of North America*. Seymour, CT: The Greenwich Workshop Press, 2006.

Geiger, Beth. *Clean Water*. New York, NY: Flash Point, 2009.

Harold, Barbara. *Catching Panfish: A Multi Species Guide*. Chanhassen, MN: Creative Publishing international, 2007.

Hearst Books. *How to Tempt a Fish*. New York, NY: Hearst Books, 2008.

Klobuchar, Lisa. *Fishing*. Chicago, IL: Heinemann Library, 2006.

Labignan, Italo. *Hook, Line and Sinker: Everything Kids Want to Know About Fishing!* Key Bolton, Ontario, Canada: Porter Books, 2007.

Le Tutla, Matt. *Professional Fishing Tips and Techniques: The Ultimate Guide*. Seattle, WA: CreateSpace, 2010.

Lilley, Tim. *Ultralight Fishing*. Chanhassen, MN: Creative Publishing international, 2005.

Parker, Steve. *Fish*. New York, NY: DK Children, 2005.

Parks, Peggy J. *Water Pollution*. Detroit, MI: KidHaven Press, 2007.

Pascoe, Elaine. *Freshwater Fish*. Detroit, MI: Blackbirch Press, 2005.

Perich, Shawn. *Catching Panfish: Tactics for Sunfish, Crappies, Yellow Perch and White Bass*. Chanhassen, MN: Creative Publishing international, 2006.

Pfeiffer, C. Boyd. *Fishing Tips & Tricks: More Than 500 Guide-Tested Tips & Tactics for Freshwater and Saltwater Angling*. Chanhassen, MN: Creative Publishing international, 2008.

Philpott, Lindsey. *Complete Book of Fishing Knots, Lines, and Leaders*. New York, NY: Skyhorse Publishing, 2008.

Smith, Delia. *Fish*. New York, NY: DK, 2006.

Underwood, Lamar. *1001 Fishing Tips: The Ultimate Guide to Finding and Catching More and Bigger Fish*. New York, NY: Skyhorse Publishing, 2010.

BIBLIOGRAPHY

Bowen, Scott. *Fishing for Everyone*. Guilford, CT: Morris Book Publishing, 2009.

Creative Publishing international. *Walleye Patterns & Presentations: How to Catch Trophy Fish in Lakes, Rivers and Reservoirs*. Chanhassen, MN: Creative Publishing international, 2001.

Evanoff, Vlad. *The Freshwater Fisherman's Bible*. New York, NY: Doubleday, 1990.

Gilbey, Henry. *Fishing*. New York, NY: DK, 2008.

Lemke, Chris. (Outdoor Connection, Two Harbors, MN) in discussion with the author, October 2010.

Lilley, Tim. *Ultralight Fishing*. Chanhassen, MN: Creative Publishing International, 2005.

Livingston, A. D. *The Freshwater Fish Cookbook: More than 200 Ways to Cook Your Catch*. Guilford, CT: Lyons Press, 2008.

Miesen, Gunnar. *Live Bait Fishing*. Chanhassen, MN: Creative Publishing international, 2005.

Minnesota Department of Natural Resources. "Crappies." 2010. Retrieved September 23, 2010 (http://www.dnr.state.mn.us/fish/crappie.html).

Minnesota Pollution Control Agency. "Let's Get the Lead Out: Non-Lead Alternatives for Fishing Tackle." 2010. Retrieved October 1, 2010 (http://www.pca.state.mn.us/index.php/living-green/living-green-citizen/household-hazardous-waste/nontoxic-tackle-let-s-get-the-lead-out.html).

North American Fishing Club. *The Ultimate Guide to Freshwater Fishing*. Boston, MA: Publishing Solutions, 2003.

Peterson, David H. (Naturalist, Two Harbors, MN) in discussion with the author, October 2010.

Recreational Boating & Fishing Foundation. "What Causes Water Pollution?" 2010. Retrieved October 1, 2010 (http://www.

takemefishing.org/general/conservation/water-pollution/
what-causes-water-pollution).

Schara, Ron. *Ron Schara's Minnesota Fishing Guide*. Golden Valley,
MN: Tristan Outdoors, 2003.

Shultz, Ken. *Ken Shultz's Essentials of Fishing*. Hoboken, NJ: John
Wiley & Sons, 2010.

Shultz, Ken. *North American Fishing*. Upper Saddle River, NJ: Creative
Outdoors, 2007.

Sorenson, Eric L. *The Angler's Guide to Freshwater Fishing*. Stillwater,
MN: Voyageur Press, 2000.

Stenberg, Dick. *Art of Freshwater Fishing*. Minnetonka, MN: Cy
DeCosse, 1985.

University of Wisconsin Sea Grant Institute. "Pumpkinseed." Accessed
September 22, 2010 (http://www.seagrant.wisc.edu/greatlakesfish/
fpumpkinseed.html).

U.S. Coast Guard. "Wearing Your Life Jacket." April 29, 2009. Retrieved
September 22, 2010 (http://www.uscgboating.org/safety/life_
jacket_wear_wearing_your_life_jacket.aspx).

U.S. Environmental Protection Agency. "What You Need to Know
About Mercury in Fish and Shellfish." June 17, 2010. Retrieved
October 1, 2010 (http://water.epa.gov/scitech/swguidance/fish
shellfish/outreach/advice_index.cfm).

INDEX

About the Author

Judy Monroe Peterson has earned two master's degrees and is the author of more than fifty educational books for young people. She is a former health care, technical, and academic librarian and college faculty member; a biologist and research scientist; and curriculum editor with more than twenty-five years of experience. She has taught courses at 3M, the University of Minnesota, and Lake Superior College. Currently, she is a writer and editor of K–12 and post-high school curriculum materials on a variety of subjects, including biology, life science, and the environment. She enjoys fishing with her family on the ponds and lakes of Minnesota.

About the Consultant

Benjamin Cowan has more than twenty years of both fresh and saltwater angling experience. In addition to being an avid outdoorsman, Cowan is also a member of many conservation organizations. He currently resides in west Tennessee.

Photo Credits

Cover, pp. 1, 3, 7, 10, 17, 20, 25, 30, 34, 41, 44, 47 Driendl Group/Photodisc/Getty Images; pp. 4–5, 7, 17, 25, 34, 44 (water) © www.istockphoto.com/Michael Jay; p. 5 Hemera/Thinkstock; pp. 8–9 Valueline/Thinkstock; pp. 13, 18–19, 32, 37, 45, 48–49, 51 © AP Images; pp. 14–15 © Drake Fleege/GreenStockMedia/The Image Works; p. 21 BRAD DOKKEN/MCT/Landov; p. 23 Steve Gorton/Dorling Kindersley/Getty Images; p. 26 iStockphoto/Thinkstock; pp. 28–29 © www.istockphoto.com/Michael Braun; p. 35 © www.istockphoto.com/Lawrence Sawyer; p. 39 © www.istockphoto.com/knape; p. 40 © www.istockphoto.com/Vincent Wallace; back cover and interior silhouettes (figures) © www.istockphoto.com/A-Digit, (grass) © www.istockphoto.com/Makhnach M.

Designer: Nicole Russo; Editor: Kathy Kuhtz Campbell;
Photo Researcher: Amy Feinberg